Praise for

Embracing Heaven & Earth

"I have always been amazed at the ability of Andrew Cohen to communicate the highest teaching, that of the ultimate truth, with the utmost simplicity. For fifty years now I have been reading books about spiritual life. *Embracing Heaven & Earth* is among the few that may truly help the ardent seeker to dissipate misunderstandings and follow a safe path."

—ARNAUD DESJARDINS,
author of *The Jump into Life: Moving beyond Fear*

"In this small book, Andrew Cohen once again challenges our spiritual sincerity. While this challenge may be shocking, *Embracing Heaven & Earth* is actually a profoundly compassionate work. Cohen's integrity and clarity about the nature of practice make it ruthlessly encouraging, a tool for inquiry and a support for purity of intention that can be returned to over and over again."

—DR. NANCY BAKER,
Dept. of Philosophy, Sarah Lawrence College

"How do you convey teachings about Enlightenment when it eludes the grasp of words and defies the hungry intellect? By the use of skillful means. In *Embracing Heaven & Earth* Andrew Cohen employs words with the precision of a diamond cutter as he operates on the minds of sentient beings, determined to reveal the lotus-jewel within."

—VERNON KITABU TURNER ROSHI,
author of *Soul Sword: The Way and Mind of a Zen Warrior*

"This is a beautiful, pure book on the high road to Enlightenment, the straight and narrow."

—T. GEORGE HARRIS,
former Editor-in-Chief of *Psychology Today* and *American Health*

"*Embracing Heaven & Earth* is both inspirational and practical. It speaks to my heart as well as my mind. It is a book of rare originality, worth savoring and studying—truly the work of a modern master."

—PATRICIA WALDEN,
Director, Boston BKS Iyengar Yoga Center

"This is a book of extraordinary spiritual intelligence, challenging the reader to participate in the ultimate revolution: to abandon the security of the known for the thrill of the unknown, which is Enlightenment. Andrew Cohen's teaching about the unconditional nature of spiritual Liberation and the responsibility of the individual to achieve it is uncompromising and profoundly disturbing to the ego. There lies its power to transform the individual who can hear him. Anyone who is not prepared to question ruthlessly the limitation, defensiveness, ignorance and cynicism of the ego, and to engage innocently with the totally unexpected, should not read this book."

–DR. LEON SCHLAMM,
Dept. of Theology and Religious Studies, University of Kent

"We recognize spiritual truth by how it resonates in our hearts. And in his compelling new book *Embracing Heaven & Earth,* Andrew Cohen touches this resonance with his usual uncompromising conviction. He reminds us that there is neither an 'up there' nor a 'down here' in spiritual growth. There is only one place—and it is within each of us. Bravo!"

–SWAMI CHETANANANDA,
Founder, Nityananda Institute, author of *The Breath of God*

"If your path is the wisdom path, Andrew Cohen's new book is a must read. When you read it you will want to do the practices he suggests for quantum leaping beyond dualism and dichotomies."

–DR. AMIT GOSWAMI,
author of *The Self-Aware Universe*

"I have an appreciation for Andrew Cohen's works on the quest of the spiritual path, which explore the essence of religious faith. His work is very beneficial for anyone curious about Enlightenment as the ultimate goal. I have confidence that *Embracing Heaven & Earth* will bring great benefit to readers and seekers in their spiritual practices."

–HIS HOLINESS PENOR RINPOCHE,
Head of the Nyingma School of Tibetan Buddhism

"A terrific book. A must for every Enlightenment library. Highly recommended. I give this book ten thumbs up."

–E. J. GOLD,
author of *The American Book of the Dead*

"To the extent that it is possible to do so in words, this deceptively small volume presents the call to Enlightenment in its nakedness. Anyone who has become comfortable with compromise and half-truth should be aware that opening these pages could be dangerous."

–Dr. James R. Lewis,
Dept. of Philosophy and Religious Studies, University of Wisconsin

"To be a spiritual path, a set of teachings must go beyond fostering a positive sense of self. Ultimately the egocentric worldview that lies at the core of human suffering must be seen for what it is. Awakening only results when the limited view of our self and life is voluntarily placed in the fire of transformation. Andrew Cohen speaks directly to this phase of the path in a voice that is bold and fresh."

–Richard Faulds,
President, Kripalu Center for Yoga and Health

"Andrew Cohen insists that 'The only way to understand what Enlightenment is, is to experience for yourself a mystery that cannot be imagined.' He offers to help. So what are you waiting for?"

–John Wren-Lewis,
School of Studies in Religion, University of Sydney

embracing
heaven
&earth

Other books by Andrew Cohen

Enlightenment Is a Secret

Freedom Has No History

An Unconditional Relationship to Life

In Defense of the Guru Principle

Who Am I? & How Shall I Live?

Autobiography of an Awakening

My Master Is My Self

embracing
heaven
&earth

the liberation teachings of
andrew cohen

MOKSHA PRESS

Moksha Press Cataloging
Cohen, Andrew, 1955 Oct. 23-
Embracing heaven & earth: the liberation teachings of Andrew Cohen.
ISBN 1-883929-29-6
[by Andrew Cohen] Foreword by John White.
1. Spiritual life 2. Egoism 3. Perfection 4. Human evolution
5. Glory of God I. Title
291.4—dc21   BL624
Library of Congress Control Number: 00-130627

contents

Embracing Heaven & Earth

From Darkness unto Light

by His Holiness Swami Chidananda
President, Divine Life Society

Such has been the hoary tradition through millennia, through countless generations down the corridor of centuries, the blazing light flaming bright has been handed down. Illumined souls have shared and transmitted their light to sincere seeking souls, illumining their hearts by a new understanding and a higher vision. Transforming this vision into experience is the seeker's responsibility, duty and privilege. In some rare cases the fullest illumination occurs spontaneously to some fortunate being. Such a being blesses the generation in which he or she happens to live and act. Andrew Cohen is one such being. He is a modern Western mystic who shines like a light in darkness.

Attaining Enlightenment, his ego vanished. Whatever Awareness was left behind was Cosmic in its nature and dimension. It embraced all. It became all and it was vibrant with the feeling of identification and empathy with each and everything that existed within this all. You may call it a cosmic state of consciousness springing out of deepest personal experience. As there was no ego it was at once impersonal experience also. The sensitive understanding that resulted gave rise to a great compassion. From this understanding and compassion arose a great wave of Love in the oceanwide heart. This understanding and compassionate love encompasses all existence and therefore it, as it were, embraces everything, as the title suggests, in all the earth and heaven too.

It is a sharing of a rare insight accompanied by a firm and uncompromising stand for the need for absolute and total dedication of one's entire being if one were to aspire after such experience.

Sivananda Ashram
Rishikesh, India
April 2000

Foreword

Suppose the book you are now holding were a textbook about a technical subject such as radiology or about an academic subject such as economics. It would probably be called *Fundamentals of. . . .*

This book is neither technical nor academic, yet it fully deserves the title *Fundamentals of Liberation* or *The A-B-Cs of Enlightenment* or *A Primer on Reality.* Whatever the title, this slender volume is a distillation of enormous wisdom about the most important thing for you—the how, what and why of spiritual freedom, unconditional happiness, the meaning of life, the truth of existence, God-realization, Enlightenment.

The wisdom in here is ancient; you will find it stated in various ways in all the world's sacred traditions. But Andrew Cohen is not simply collecting it as if this were a term paper. The clarity, simplicity and integrity of his teaching demonstrate that what he says is genuinely his own realization of the timeless teachings. Moreover, he articulates it in a unique, powerful expression of great value for our time.

The truth about "embracing heaven and earth" must be rediscovered by each generation if it is to be useful guidance rather than a dead weight of authority. Andrew's graceful presentation of the fundamentals of Liberation offers the kind of useful guidance so badly needed for a global society of increasing conflict and violence. "Conflict and violence" because religious groups tend to narrowly and jealously guard their piece of the truth rather than lovingly sharing it with others who likewise have their particular perspective on the nature of God and ultimate reality, which is no less true but no more comprehensive. Andrew brings those groups' fundamentals together in a way that contributes to deepened understanding by showing that the core truth of each is the same for them all.

Christians, for example, are instructed in the Bible by Jesus to "Seek ye first the kingdom of God." Andrew says, "For one who is sincerely interested in being free in this life, the simplicity inherent in wanting only Liberation and nothing else is very attractive," and he makes clear that "salvation" can only be properly understood as Liberation or Enlightenment.

Hindus, for another example, are instructed in the Bhagavad Gita to "Perform all your actions with your heart fixed on God; renounce attachment to the fruit of your actions." Andrew says, "And in the end, there is nothing more that any of us can do than want to be free more than anything else and be willing to back it up with action and with sacrifice."

Buddhists are instructed that the root cause of suffering is desire. Andrew says, "It's only when the wanting falls away that we can begin to experience a fullness that is always there."

Jews are instructed that Job's suffering and sorrows are not to be understood in personal terms because there is transcendent power and law undergirding creation. "Then the Lord answered Job out of the whirlwind, and said . . . 'Where wast thou when I laid the foundations of the earth?'" Andrew says, "Indeed, to succeed in liberating ourselves from ignorance and delusion, we have to get to that point where we're able to directly perceive the impersonal nature of every aspect of our own personal experience."

These are some of the fundamentals of Liberation. But rather than you finding them piecemeal here and there in other sources, Andrew's realization of the truth of existence synthesizes them in a seamless and refreshing style. Stunning insights abound, wrapped in clear prose.

The truth of our existence is usually stated by enlightened teachers in terms fitted to the individual person. Andrew does that, but appropriately for us moderns in a scientifically oriented society, he places his teaching in a context of evolutionary development for the entire human race, as well as in a context of cosmic laws that impersonally operate and influence us as individuals and as a species. Most important of all and wholly in accord with the highest collective wisdom of the world's sacred traditions, he emphasizes that Enlightenment is to be attained not simply for oneself but for everyone, because the spiritual unity of humankind means that as long as one person is not free, no one is free.

Andrew uses the term "spiritual warrior," which I especially appreciate because it connotes the one-pointed, fierce, steadfast dedication that the best warriors have as they go into battle—an attitude of "no surrender–no retreat," which mobilizes the warrior's entire resources to attain victory. It was the attitude of the Buddha on the night he sat beneath the bodhi tree and vowed not to leave until he attained Enlightenment or died; it was the attitude of Jesus when he entered Jerusalem prior to his crucifixion. Such people, upon attaining Enlightenment, become what I call "RAMBO-dhisattvas," that is, peace warriors of great skill and wisdom who will not cease their loving efforts on behalf of ignorant, self-deluded humanity until all have attained Enlightenment.

Although I have never met Andrew except through his teachings, I regard him as a RAMBO-dhisattva. I am not a devotee of his or even a member of his community; I am simply a supporter of Truth wherever I find it. In the teachings of Andrew Cohen, I find important guidance for modern spiritual seekers. I commend it to you for your spiritual health and growth.

JOHN WHITE
author of *The Meeting of Science and Spirit* and *What Is Enlightenment?*

Introduction

Andrew Cohen is a dangerous man, and this is a dangerous book. Dangerous to our cynicism, dangerous to despair and hopelessness, dangerous to any willingness to compromise what we know to be right or true. If the search for truth has become obscured by doubt, the goal of freedom slipping into the far distant future, you can find here the immediacy of a living teaching—living now, in your experience. The teachings in this book show us how to find out for ourselves, from our own experience, what it means to be a human being. They challenge any complacency or unexamined assumptions in our spiritual practice or knowledge. They speak only to that part of ourselves that holds a spark of hope for human goodness, that quickens every time someone even says the word "freedom," that yearns and yearns like an unrequited lover for some meaning to life that is bigger, deeper, all-consuming. On every page, the words cry "yes!" to the utterly thrilling possibility that life can make perfect and absolutely beautiful sense and that we each can be a force of human evolution itself. This book is a Book of Life, your life and LIFE writ large.

This is not a book of ideas or concepts or commentaries about truths glimpsed through the dark mirror of the mind. It is the living experience of one man, Andrew Cohen. Yet simply and most profoundly, it is a testament to our deepest shared human experience. Andrew's radical message is, as the title of this book implies, that heaven can be brought to earth—and, in fact, that it is our sacred duty to do so. He shows us how to live the glory revealed in our most profound spiritual experiences by harnessing their liberating power as a force for radical transformation and evolution itself. Nothing is required—no special initiation, no complicated techniques, no obscure systems of knowledge. Just being a human being fully immersed in the fundamental predicament of wondering who we are in this cosmos, and what to do on this planet. In this extraordinary book is everything we need to live our earthly lives fueled by the fire of heaven.

So who *is* Andrew Cohen? He's a revolutionary spiritual teacher whose weapons are a razor-sharp inquiry into what's true and a devastating passion for the transformation of the human race. He is the sworn enemy of ego, a liberator of the human heart. Andrew's consistent stand for freedom—his daring pursuit of the truth in any situation, his demand that we realize and live a love that has no bounds—shows us that victory is possible. He urges us to leap into the fire of our deepest passion, to burn, to care more and more until the whole world explodes in our hearts. His war cry, his love that takes no prisoners, sends a shock wave against the mediocrity and cynicism where ego thrives.

Not unlike revolutionary teachers of the past, Andrew's own search for truth has led him beyond the prevailing wisdom of our time into a dynamic inquiry that truly does embrace both heaven and earth. Over the fifteen years since he began guiding others on the path to Liberation, Andrew has engaged himself in a remarkable apprenticeship to the human condition. He has tirelessly and ceaselessly explored what it is that holds us back from living the truth of what we discover in our deepest spiritual experiences. A rare teaching is the result—what Andrew calls *Impersonal Enlightenment*. Taking us beyond our blinding self-preoccupation, this teaching of Impersonal Enlightenment brings us to a tangible recognition of our shared human experience, a recognition that urgently demands that we do everything we possibly can to transform the ignorance and division in ourselves and the world. What is radical and revolutionary about Enlightenment, Andrew teaches, is that it is an impersonal force for the evolution of humanity as a whole. This is the context for the teachings in this book.

Here Andrew has crystallized his fundamental teachings into five tenets. These tenets are tools to help us uncover the mystery and mechanics of our own experience. When experienced in depth, they are also revealed to be actual spiritual laws that live already in each of us, waiting for their power to be released. Nothing of what we usually identify as our personal selves—our thoughts, feelings and history—has relevance to these tenets or to the order of being that they reveal. They are perfectly empty of the personal, separate sense of self. They destroy the need for psychology as we know it, revealing our romance with personal drama to be nothing more than a trick of the mind that keeps us from recognizing the glory and deadly seriousness of our lives. These tenets and the other essential teachings presented in this book starve the ego, forcing it to let go of its death grip on our hearts, allowing the awesome fire of our True Self to begin to animate our every breath.

Don't underestimate the power of what is in this book. Andrew dares to present a radical psychology of Liberation that takes us far beyond who and what we recognize ourselves to be. While the mind can appreciate the perfect logic of these compelling words, they are not simply words but *experience* captured in black and white. They are a direct current into the unknown depth of human being. Sincere contemplation of these teachings—an attentive dialogue between your experience and these words—will provide access to an astonishing self-knowledge. Pay attention to what moves in you, listen for the call that dares to take you beyond the established territory of the known. Something far greater is happening here, an explosion in creation itself, a potential for human being that ends the strife-filled world that we know. Beyond desire, beyond the personal, an unknown potential that is Life unbridled awaits us. It waits for you on the pages of this book.

DR. ELIZABETH DEBOLD
author of *Mother Daughter Revolution*

The Five Fundamental
Tenets of Enlightenment

Clarity of Intention

The Law of Volitionality

Face Everything and Avoid Nothing

The Truth of Impersonality

For the Sake of the Whole

These five tenets define what an enlightened relationship to the human experience is. They describe simply and clearly how to live what is discovered in the spiritual revelation—how to embody the absolute nature of that revelation in the life that we are living here and now. If we are truly sincere in our desire to manifest the precious jewel of Liberation in this life, then these five tenets must be lived without conditions, at all times, in all places, through all circumstances.

the first tenet
Clarity of Intention

If you want to be free, if you want to be a liberated human being, then it is essential that you become interested in what it means to be simple—terrifyingly simple, frighteningly simple, shockingly simple.

For many of us, simplicity is not easy to understand. The notion of simplicity in relationship to what it means to be a human being is a concept that is very alien to us— alien not only intellectually but also experientially. To many of us, simplicity doesn't even sound attractive. Usually what we're attracted to is the very opposite of that which is simple. But simplicity is where our salvation lies. And if we want to be free, if we want to become truly sane human beings, then it is essential to look deeply into what it means to become simple.

The movement from bondage to Liberation is the movement from complexity to simplicity. And this movement, the movement from complexity to simplicity, will in the end require the renunciation of all that is false, wrong and untrue. It will demand the willingness to transcend all that is superficial and irrelevant. You see, so much of what we're interested in and preoccupied with, from a deeply spiritual perspective, will ultimately be revealed to be completely irrelevant, without importance and a total waste of time.

If we want to become simple, then instead of wanting many things, as most of us do, we have to come to that point where we want only *one thing*. That's all there is to it. If we want to be free, if we want to be able to experience what it means to be a liberated human being, the way to that attainment can be found simply through ceasing to want many things and wanting only one thing.

If we want only one thing and that is Liberation alone, then our vision becomes clear and distinct and our attention becomes very focused. Why? Because we want only *one thing.* And it's difficult to be confused when we want only one thing. You see, when we want many things it's very easy to be confused. But if we want only one thing, and this *never* changes for any reason at any time, we will discover an undreamed-of clarity of being. We will be free from fundamental confusion because our attention will always be focused on Liberation alone and nowhere else.

For one who is sincerely interested in being free in this life, the simplicity inherent in wanting only Liberation and nothing else is very attractive. For that individual, just the thought of wanting only to be free, just the conviction that *nothing else matters,* in and of itself, is profoundly liberating. Wanting only to be free—and being willing to exclude anything and everything else from our attention—liberates us from the world. Wanting to be free more than anything else liberates us from the mind and from time. It really does. It not only frees us from the endless burden of having so many choices, but it releases us from the often compelling attraction to all that is false, wrong and untrue.

So if we want to be free more than anything else, then we become very simple. If Liberation is the only thing that is important to us, and we're willing to back it up with action in such a way that we will not succumb to the temptation to believe that anything else could ever be more important, then we become quite simple indeed. To a very worldly person, to someone who has no sense of the spiritual dimension of life, we may have become unbearably simple, appallingly simple. He or she may even feel that we have gone too far and have started to take this whole matter of Liberation much too seriously. Why? Because we are not deeply interested in anything else. Nothing else moves us, nothing else inspires us, nothing else touches us.

Now it's important to understand that those who have come to the place that I just described—those who cannot be swayed in any way from their one-pointed interest in liberating themselves from fear and ignorance in this life—

find that they have a lot in common with one who has actually succeeded. They have a lot in common with someone who has become a living, breathing manifestation of the kind of simplicity that I have been speaking about. You see, someone who *wants* to be free more than anything else and one who *is* free are in many ways not all that different. If you want to be free more than anything else, and if you're willing to make any sacrifice in order to succeed in winning the prize of Liberation in this life, then from a certain point of view *you've already won.*

Of course we don't know how many of us are actually going to succeed in becoming enlightened in this life. We can never predict these things. But the question of how many of us are going to come to that point in our own evolution where we are willing to do *anything that we possibly can* in order to succeed is a very different matter. You see, the power to go that far lies in our very own hands. And in the end, there is nothing more that any of us can do than want to be free more than anything else and be willing to back it up with action and with sacrifice. From a certain point of view, whether or not we actually succeed in becoming fully enlightened doesn't really matter. It doesn't make any difference. But what does make all the difference in the world is whether or not we are *truly willing now.*

If we are truly willing now, our relationship to the whole world and everything in it changes—*all things become possible*. Why? Because inwardly our attention has become one-pointed. It is now focused upon a mystery in which there exists no sense of limitation whatsoever. This mystery is immeasurable, indescribable, unknowable. But when our attention is primarily focused on the material world—on what we want from it, how we feel about it and what we think about it—all things are *no longer* possible because we have given our attention entirely to that which is inherently limited. And when our attention has been given entirely to that which is inherently limited, very little is possible. You see, there is no room for that depth that has no limit when life is lived without any knowledge or experience of a miraculous possibility—without any knowledge of that which is sacred, of that which is perfect always because that is its nature. A life that is lived without any knowledge or experience of that possibility is a life of limitation, and limitation in relationship to the freedom I'm speaking about is the same as no life at all.

It's important to understand that, in the end, all any of us can do is want to be free more than anything else and be willing to do anything necessary in order to succeed. When we've come to that point where we are literally doing everything that we possibly can, when we are ceaselessly extending ourselves, fully and without reservation, and in that wanting only to die, then and only then will there be nothing more for us to do. And then and only then will we begin to discover what Liberation actually is. You see, our attention only needs to be on doing anything and everything we possibly can in order to succeed. If we are willing to do this fully, unconditionally and without reservation, then *in that we will be saved.* We will actually experience salvation. Whatever else may or may not occur is really beyond our control. We do not have a say in it. Beyond this unconditional willingness to die there is just a mystery, and how it works we will never know.

Wanting to be free more than anything else means that we have stopped waiting. It means that we have stopped procrastinating. It means that we have stopped deceiving ourselves and that we have finally become serious. It means that having an unconditional relationship to freedom is no longer something that frightens us. On the contrary, it sets our hearts on fire.

For spiritual experience to lead to extraordinary transformation, we must be deeply grounded in an unshakable desire to become liberated. That means that we must be willing to leave this world and everyone in it behind forever. Unless we are, there is going to be a return, which means we are going to come back. We are going to come back because we are not sure that we want to be free more than anything else. Free means FREE. Free means leaving *everything* behind. Freedom means having nothing and having nothing *is* freedom. You must understand that Enlightenment is not an object that the ego, the separate sense of self, can play with for its own amusement.

So for spiritual practice to bear the fruit of Liberation, it must be inspired by an unshakable intention to succeed at any cost. To be able to liberate us from fear, ignorance and a profoundly self-centered relationship to life, spiritual practice must be inspired by a burning passion to go all the way. Without this burning passion, it will not have the power to liberate. In fact, spiritual practice, in any context other than that of Liberation alone, may even become the enemy. Why? Because it will in all likelihood enable the ego to feel better about itself. And in that, there is the great danger that we may lose touch with the overwhelming sense of urgency that is so essential if anything is really going to change.

What I am speaking about is the very foundation of my teaching. It is also, I believe, the foundation of any genuine teaching of Enlightenment. The path, the goal and everything in between begin and end with this and this alone. I call it *Clarity of Intention.* It is a fundamental and absolute resolution to be free *in this life. Clarity of Intention* means that we want to be free more than anything else *here and now.* Here and now means that in relationship to any choice that we make, to any action that we take, in relationship to any event that may have occurred in the past or may occur in the future, first and foremost *we want to be free.* Wanting to be free changes everything. Look into this for yourself and you'll see how true it is.

In light of the intention to be free, all things become clear. *Clarity of Intention* is the most direct path out of deep and fundamental confusion. Indeed, the intention to be free, when sufficiently cultivated, has the unique power to penetrate the often overwhelming illusion created by all that is personal. It can cut through the illusion of blinding complexity created by our attachment to self-importance in an instant, if only we are willing. But its demand is absolute. The intention to be free, when taken seriously, demands everything from us—and then a little bit more. It cannot be taken lightly. You see, the only reason that those who begin on the path do not succeed, indeed, the only reason that they make important mistakes, is that *they were not true to the one-pointed desire to be free more than anything else.* If we are always true to the desire to be free, we won't make important mistakes—it won't be possible. If we're always true to that and that alone, we cannot fail.

But if we are not true to the urgency of this call to Liberation, if we allow ourselves to get distracted, if we allow ourselves to believe that anything else could ever be more important, the delicate confidence that is the very foundation of the path will fall to pieces. Without being aware of it, we will allow ourselves to be casual. Then, in a flash, the liberating power of inner certainty and unwavering conviction will be gone.

You see, this kind of passion, this intensity of interest, cannot be taken for granted. In this world, where there is so much distraction and where our attention is usually painfully focused upon a self-centered and deeply materialistic relationship to life, the delicacy and preciousness of this kind of passion is almost completely unknown. Indeed, in this world, the passion for freedom will not survive within us unless we are deadly serious, unusually vigilant and extremely careful. That's just the way it is.

It's so easy to deceive ourselves. In fact, it's the easiest thing to do. Most people do it all the time. What is ignorance? *Ignorance is a state of constant self-deception.* It is so rare that a human being actually wakes up for more than a few moments. And it is because of the intensity of this habit of living in a self-deceived way that it is essential to be absolutely one-pointed about Liberation. Unless we become one-pointed, we are not going to make it. The forces against us and the currents of ignorance in the world that we live in are just too strong.

To understand *Clarity of Intention* for oneself is to understand the meaning and the significance of simplicity. I strongly encourage you to contemplate the implications of simplicity, of *absolute* simplicity. If you do this, you will get a very clear sense of exactly what it is that I am pointing to. Go into this over and over and over again. Go into this absolute simplicity so deeply that you begin to feel and know directly, know *experientially,* exactly what it is that I am pointing to. And when you experientially get in touch with what simplicity actually means, you can then begin to look into its opposite, which is complexity. Then everything will be revealed to you. All will become clear—the difference between wisdom and ignorance, freedom and bondage, heaven and hell. When seen from the perspective of simplicity, complexity and all it represents begins to look and feel extremely unattractive and very painful. In fact, complexity is now experienced as the essence of that which is confusing, deluding and inherently divided. But you have to discover this for yourself.

Look into simplicity. Look deeply into it. And when you find a simplicity that is so simple that it is absolute, keep your attention there. It is in that absolute simplicity that the truth is found. Those who don't have the eyes to see are dazzled by complexity. They often believe that in complexity there is inherent significance. But don't be fooled. It's really the other way around.

If you want to be able to know directly and experientially what the truth is, then you have to become simple first. The reason for this is that *complexity cannot understand simplicity.* But—and this is the whole point—simplicity *can* understand complexity. Complexity cannot see simplicity, but simplicity *can* see complexity. In order to get in touch with the source of all true wisdom *you have to become simple yourself.* It just doesn't work the other way around. You see, simplicity means being whole. It means being perfectly undivided, *completely unified.*

I strongly urge you to give as much of your attention as you can to looking into this. I cannot emphasize enough how important it is. The absolute simplicity that can be discovered and experienced directly through the one-pointed contemplation of the desire for freedom above anything else *is* Liberation. That is why intense and profound contemplation of the first tenet, *Clarity of Intention,* is so important. Indeed, that is why the one-pointed contemplation of the desire for freedom alone is the most important part of the spiritual life.

the second tenet
The Law of Volitionality

The second tenet, *The Law of Volitionality,* is very challenging. It states that if we want to be free, we have to be willing to assume absolute responsibility for everything that we do. The reason that *The Law of Volitionality* is such a challenging teaching is that we live in a world where most of us are convinced that we couldn't possibly be responsible for everything that we do. And the reason we believe we couldn't possibly be responsible for everything that we do is simply that we are convinced that we are victims—*victims who are out of control.*

I discovered something very extraordinary early on in my teaching career. I discovered that on a deep level *we all know exactly what we are doing.* What does that mean? It means that people who want to be happy make choices that enable them to experience happiness. And people who do not want to be happy deliberately make choices that ensure the continuation of their experience of unhappiness. For those of us seeking spiritual Liberation, the same rule applies.

These days many are saying that they want to be free, but if that is true, why is it that so few of us can honestly claim victory over ignorance? The second tenet, *The Law of Volitionality*, states that everything is volitional, including our relationship to liberation from fear, ignorance and selfishness. The fact is, those who say they want to be free more than anything else and *mean it* actually succeed. And that is because they accept unconditionally the validity of *The Law of Volitionality*. That means they are willing to wholeheartedly take responsibility for absolutely everything that they do.

Often when spiritual seekers speak about their internal experience, they have an interesting habit—they refer to different "parts" of themselves. They say that there is one part that wants to be free and there is another part that does not. Some even report that there are different "voices" speaking to them inside their own heads—one voice expressing a passionate interest in freedom and the other voice very much opposed to the idea.

Now when we find different voices speaking within us—one pulling us in the direction of Liberation and another pushing us in the very opposite direction—it does *appear* that there is more than one of us in there. But the all-important fact that so many of us seem to miss is that there is always only *one* who hears these different voices—

one entity, one individual, one self. Indeed, there is only *one experiencer* who hears both the call to Liberation *and* the voice of doubt, that voice that continually insists that it's not really possible to be free. Not possible for whom? For that very same *one self* who hears the call to Liberation. Again, there is only one self who responds to the call to Liberation. And it is that very same one self who seems to fall into the clutches of our darkest impulses time and time again.

It is very important to recognize this. What I'm speaking about seems obvious when described in this way. But it is definitely *not* obvious to most of us when we are in the midst of confusion, when we are directly experiencing these contradictory impulses within us—one toward heaven and the other toward hell.

Now the reason there appear to be different parts of ourselves is only that we are in the habit of making choices that follow these extremely contradictory impulses within us. When we choose that which is positive, the self that chooses experiences that which is positive. When we choose that which is negative, the self that chooses experiences that which is negative. Indeed, when we choose freedom, when we choose liberation from ignorance and selfishness, we experience a sense of self that is so positive that it shatters all the concepts we ever had about what the word *positive* means. And when we choose that which is negative, we instantly experience a sense of self that is inherently separate, ambitious and driven by fear.

Because there is a qualitative difference in the way these different choices make the one self *feel,* we unknowingly presume that there is more than one self within us. But there is not. There is only one self, one experiencer, who is either experiencing that which is positive or that which is negative *due to the choice that that one self has made.* So therefore, what self are we choosing to manifest? What self are we choosing to be? There is only one self within us. And that one self *becomes what it chooses.*

The reason that we suffer incessantly, the reason that the painful experience of isolation and separation is so common, is in fact only because we don't make the right choices. Why don't we make the right choices? The traditional answer is that due to our state of ignorance, we don't know any better. And until that all-important turning point in our own evolution when we make the momentous decision to be *free,* to be liberated in this life, ignorance will always be a valid excuse for making the wrong choices. But *after* we make the conscious decision to be liberated in this life, *ignorance will never again be a reasonable excuse for making the wrong choices* because if the choice to be free has been made in good conscience, from that moment on, deep in our hearts we will always know exactly what we are doing.

Now the most difficult choice for us to make is the choice to be responsible for everything that we do. Most of us do not want to get anywhere near that kind of relationship to life. It's just too big. It's just too much. Only those individuals who have absolutely no doubt that they want to be free, enlightened human beings will be interested. Most of us don't want to assume this degree of responsibility. Why? It's very simple. Because then we would no longer be able to place the burden of blame for our own misery upon anyone else. We don't want to give up the idea that we are victims, that we have been "hard done by." We don't want to give up the deeply held conviction that we need time to heal our wounds, that we need more time to overcome the past, that we need even more time to continue to live a life of compromise. You see, *perfection is not what we're interested in.* What does perfection mean? It means taking unconditional responsibility for ourselves in the name of Liberation *here and now.* But *perfection* is a word that we don't want to get near. It makes us feel as if we can't breathe. And if a word like perfection causes us to experience a sense of suffocation rather than great inspiration, then it can only mean that we are deeply invested in and attached to being less than that.

Indeed, words like *absolute* and *perfect* challenge to the ultimate degree every single part of us that does not want to be free, every part of us that desperately wants to remain separate. And if words like absolute and perfect disturb us, then we need to look deeply into the true nature of our relationship to life. If we do, we will probably find that the attraction that we have to that which is sacred is divided. And that means that at those times when we are under enormous pressure, when our back is against the wall, that voice within us that doesn't want to be free, that doesn't want perfection, is going to demand, in no uncertain terms, room for itself.

As long as we allow ourselves to be divided in this way, it will never be possible to be free. And that is the only reason that so few actually succeed. Most of us are far more committed to maintaining the freedom to be *separate,* the freedom to *not* be fully responsible for ourselves, than we are to attaining Liberation here and now. The fact is that most of us do not want to rid ourselves of this fundamental division.

In our internal experience, before the eye of our mind, numerous possibilities arise and pass away in every moment—numerous possibilities and also numerous *choices.* So once again the question is: What choices are we making? As I said earlier, if you look deeply enough within your own self, you're going to discover that there is only one of you, not many, and that the choices that you make define the very identity of that one self within you. Indeed, *it is the choices that we make and those choices alone that define who we actually are in any given moment,* and from one moment to another who we are can change radically. But this is the good news—profound and radical liberation from ignorance always exists as a living possibility in every moment.

So therefore, we have to ask ourselves: What choice am I making in every moment? When we look into that question, everything becomes simple and obvious—as a matter of fact, everything becomes shockingly simple and terrifyingly obvious. That's when we discover for ourselves that there is an enormous burden that must be carried by any man or woman who is awake, any man or woman who is truly conscious of the fact that he or she is alive. So we ask ourselves: What choice am I making? Do the choices that I make express a love for the truth, a preference for that which is sacred? Or do the choices that I make demonstrate attachment to falsehood and identification with that which is unwholesome?

What I'm saying is this: To be ignorant means that we are compulsively making the wrong choices in a blind and deeply conditioned way. To be awake means that we are constantly making the right choices. Why? Because we can *see.* Because we know what it is that we are doing and why we are doing it. And because now at the very core of our being *we no longer want to make the wrong choices.* When we no longer want to make the wrong choices, we have finally been purified of the desire to choose ego, to choose separation. It is then that we begin to see directly for ourselves how the law of karma actually works.

When we make the wrong choices over and over and over again, a karmic momentum is created. It's the accumulated momentum of having made unwholesome choices consistently over a long period of time. When we have chosen selfishness and separation hundreds of thousands of times, it eventually becomes a powerful momentum, a momentum that literally becomes *self-generating*. When it becomes self-generating, that momentum begins to usurp the energy of the personality, ultimately taking control of it, propelling it forward in time. But the point is, *we* created this momentum. We created it by the choices that we made over and over and over again. That's why we so often say, "But I couldn't help it!" You see, the karmic force of this momentum has gained so much energy that it actually *seems* as if we couldn't help it. It literally appears to be happening by itself, *but only because of all the momentum behind it that has been accumulated over time.*

To be a truly liberated individual, this momentum must be completely destroyed, utterly and perfectly extinguished forever. You see, *only when this momentum has been destroyed will one have realized a state of permanent Liberation.* And the way the destruction of that powerful momentum occurs is simply through *making the choice to be free*. Making the choice to be free not only once or twice, but over and over and over again. If we want to be free, if we want to destroy the accumulated momentum of past karma, *consistency is everything.* And in order to succeed, we must develop a deep confidence in our own ability to continuously make the choice to be free, whether it *feels* like the right thing to do or not.

Often when people begin spiritual practice in earnest, they encounter this force of karma, this momentum of conditioning, and begin to do battle with it. And they usually experience enormous resistance. Resistance to what? *To doing the right thing.* Many believe that spiritual experience, in and of itself, will liberate them from the chains of karma. But the fact is, it usually does not, and this is because of the tremendous power of the accumulated karmic momentum. Spiritual experience may indeed enable us to directly perceive the true and right relationship of all things. But it is making the right choices that makes it possible for us to *act* upon that revelation. And it is through acting upon that which has been revealed to us in profound spiritual experience over and over and over again that the powerful momentum of karma can eventually be destroyed.

To succeed, we must be convinced beyond any doubt from our own experience that Liberation is a living possibility, that it is *real*. But from that moment on, whether that which was directly experienced in the spiritual revelation is apparent or not, we must *choose* to be free in every moment *no matter what.* That's when we become true spiritual warriors. That's when we have finally become serious about attaining victory over ignorance in this life.

The second tenet, *The Law of Volitionality,* states that we alone are always making the choice to be free—or to be unfree. It states that if we *do* want to be free, it is essential that we come to that point in our own evolution where we are determined only to make the right choice—the choice that will bring us to Liberation.

In the same way that the negative momentum of karma becomes self-generating as a result of making the wrong choice countless times, through the experience of revelation and, most important of all, through making the *right* choice over and over and over again, this momentum begins to slow down and our confidence in the possibility of Liberation increases. As that confidence becomes steady, it gets easier to make the right choices. And as our confidence increases even more, as a result of consistently making the right choices, the momentum of karma continues to decrease until it not only ceases altogether but—and this is everything—*a new momentum is born.*

That new momentum is the energy of Liberation itself. If pursued until the very end, that energy also becomes self-generating. Self-generating means without effort. This is a spontaneous condition, a natural state. This is when the energy of Liberation itself has overtaken the personality. *That is Liberation*—when the unconditioned, uncontainable energy of that which is Absolute, perfectly mysterious and all-knowing reveals itself in this world. What remains is the same body, the same nervous system, the same mind, but now expressing something completely other, something so miraculous that it no longer has any memory of what came before.

the third tenet

Face Everything and Avoid Nothing

The third tenet is called *Face Everything and Avoid Nothing*. It states that if we want to be free, we must be willing to face everything and avoid nothing at all times, in all places, through all circumstances.

Very few of us face anything. Without being aware of it, we are in the grip of a fear-driven habit, a habit of avoidance and denial. That habit is the movement of ego. The movement of ego is a compulsive need to remain separate at all times, in all places, through all circumstances. And as long as we are blind to this movement of ego, we will be oblivious to the enormous degree to which we are avoiding and denying any information about our own experience that would in any way conflict with the ego's compulsive need to see itself as being separate.

Once again, ego is that movement of mind that needs to maintain a separate sense of self at all times, in all places, through all circumstances. And in that movement, we will deliberately choose to avoid anything that would challenge the ultimate validity of the ego's separate identity. For the individual lost in the nightmare of ignorance, the survival of that separate sense of self always appears to be more important than anything else.

But if we have made up our minds that we want to be free, then the whole picture changes. Now the primary object of our attention is the desire for freedom, not the survival of the ego. Now we've decided that we want to be liberated from the painful experience of having our attention constantly fixated on the ego. We have discovered that as long as our attention is primarily focused upon this one object, our experience will be one of suffocation and limitation.

In the startling shift of perspective experienced in the spiritual revelation, our attention is temporarily liberated from ego fixation and as a result literally expands in all directions. In that expansion we discover something extraordinary and profound—*the true and right relationship of all things.* In the spiritual revelation, we recognize that that mysterious knowledge has always been there but because so much of our attention has been focused on the needs of the ego, we simply have been unaware of it.

We will never be able to perceive the true and right relationship of all things as long as so much of our attention is devoted to maintaining and sustaining a painfully separate sense of self. But once we are no longer invested in maintaining that sense of isolation and separation, then and only then will we be able to directly experience what it means to see clearly. In order to experience what it means to be awake, in order to be able to see clearly for ourselves what the truth actually is, we *must* liberate ourselves from the insidious need to always see ourselves as being separate.

Now if we have spent a lifetime devoting almost all of our energy to supporting the ego, while simultaneously avoiding anything that would cause us to doubt its validity, it's going to require nothing less than a heroic degree of interest, determination and passion to liberate our attention from its influence. Only if we want to be free more than anything else, and only if we have recognized the entirely volitional relationship that we have to our experience, will it be possible to override the ego's compulsive tendency to avoid and deny so much of what is actually there.

So once again, *only if the first two tenets are being lived in earnest* will we become so conscious that we will be able to directly perceive the true and right relationship of all things. Indeed, when the first two tenets are lived in earnest, instead of seeing only what the ego wants us to see, we will be able to recognize what the true picture actually is.

In the spiritual experience, the third tenet, *Face Everything and Avoid Nothing,* is recognized as being the natural expression of a liberated state of consciousness. Why? *Because in the liberated state there is no longer any desire to avoid anything.* In that state there is no longer any motivation to deny anything. In that state there is no motivation left to see things other than as they actually are.

When consciousness is liberated from the veil of ego, it's thrilling. It's thrilling because instantly there is infinite depth, extraordinary vastness and the recognition of a profound interrelatedness within a context that is limitless. Only when we allow our attention to become that vast are we going to be able to live in a way that will be a clear reflection of that vastness. How is this achieved? By facing everything and avoiding nothing at all times, in all places, through all circumstances. By *always* facing everything and avoiding nothing, and *never* for any reason swerving from that absolute relationship to our experience—*not even for an instant.*

What does it really mean to face everything and avoid nothing? It means we have to ceaselessly inquire into the true nature of what it is that is motivating us to make the choices that we make. Do we have the humility to face into the aggressive and frighteningly selfish nature of many of our own actions? Do we have that kind of courage? Because if we refuse to face the darkest parts of ourselves, we will never be able to transcend them. Only if we truly want to be free more than anything else will we find the integrity of interest that will enable us to face everything and avoid nothing, no matter how difficult or challenging it may be.

But facing everything means facing *everything*, not only

our darkest impulses. Facing everything means daring to face wholeheartedly into the infinite depth of our own Self, a depth that reveals a mystery so awe-inspiring that it simply cannot be imagined. Facing everything means facing into our own infinite potential. But more often than not, we're unwilling to do that. We're unwilling to face the profoundly liberating implications of our own potential because we're simply not prepared to accept that which our mind cannot comprehend. Always living in denial of our darkness and ever fearful of the overwhelming brightness of our own unexplored heights, the inevitable result can only be mediocrity.

Why do we have so much trouble seeing things clearly? Why do we consistently make important mistakes? The answer is simple. If we are not paying attention, we are not going to see clearly. And if we are not seeing clearly, we are not going to do the right thing. But if we want to be free more than anything else, we are going to be profoundly attentive. You see, in order to do the right thing we want to see the whole picture, which is the true and right relationship of all things. When we make important mistakes, when we consistently do the wrong thing, it simply means that we weren't paying attention. And the only reason we don't pay attention is that we don't want to be free more than anything else.

If you understand this very deeply, the mysterious question of how to *live* the spiritual experience can be easily understood. Believe it or not, the third tenet is literally the means to your own perfect Liberation. But you have to recognize this for yourself. Then the path in all its glory will reveal itself before your very own eyes. When that happens, you will know without any doubt that even you can be free in this life, if only you are willing to pay the price.

the fourth tenet
The Truth of Impersonality

The fourth tenet is called *The Truth of Impersonality*. This tenet states that every aspect of our personal experience is a *completely impersonal affair.*

The teaching of impersonality reveals the ultimately impersonal nature of *all* human experience and can enable any human being who wants to be free more than anything else to gain a rare degree of objectivity in relationship to the ever-confusing arena of personal experience. Because it is in the subjective or personal domain of our experience that we so easily become lost and confused, if we want to be free it is essential that we find a way to understand our personal experience from a perspective that is inherently objective. What enables a human being to experience for him- or herself the liberating clarity of objectivity in relationship to all that is personal is the direct perception of the ultimately impersonal nature of all human experience.

Now I think it can be said that unless we sincerely want to be free, it's going to be very difficult, if not impossible, to even begin to become aware of the impersonal nature of our own experience. *The Truth of Impersonality* states that the human experience could never be uniquely yours, mine or anyone else's. And *impersonal* points to the fact that ultimately all human experience is one, and the true nature of that experience is not personal.

Everyone experiences fear at one time or another. When you experience fear, when I experience fear, when anyone experiences fear, what is felt is exactly the same. If you were to enter my body when I was experiencing fear, or if I were to enter your body when you were experiencing fear, or indeed, if we were to enter anyone's body when there was the presence of fear, we would discover that there is no difference whatsoever in the *feeling* experience itself. There may be some difference in the degree of intensity with which the feeling is experienced, but the presence of fear, the feeling of fear itself, is one and the same. *The whole point is that there is only one experience of fear.* In the same way, when we experience sexual feelings, the feeling experience of lust is exactly the same for each and every one of us. Again, there may be different degrees of intensity, but the fundamental feeling of that experience is one and the same for all.

The arena of spiritual experience is no different. A yearning for transcendence, a longing for Liberation, is a manifestation of an *impersonal* evolutionary impulse. Many people experience the movement of this impulse at different times in their lives. The awakening of the desire for transcendence within the individual is an expression of the evolutionary impulse within the race as a whole. The movement of this impulse is not unique, in the sense that when one individual experiences that longing, it's not, at the level of feeling, different from the experience of another who also feels the movement of that longing. Once again, there may be profound differences in the intensity of that movement, but the feeling experience itself is exactly the same.

As I said in the previous chapters, there is an enormous amount of momentum that has been generated through a blind and compulsive drive to see oneself as being separate. This drive is what ego is. The most significant component of this compulsion is the need to see our own personal feeling experience as somehow *different, special and unique.* Through the ongoing experiential recognition of the impersonal nature of all feeling experience, it becomes increasingly difficult to believe that our own experience could really be as unique or different as we had imagined it to be. In fact, it is in that recognition that the very mechanism of ego can be seen for what it is. Simply put, *the need to personalize is ego.* And the destruction of ego occurs when the need to personalize falls away.

It is no easy task to come to the end of a personal relationship to our own experience. In fact, it's simply too much for most of us to bear. The implications are far too radical. To move from a very personal relationship with our own experience to one that is deeply impersonal requires an enormous leap. In order to actually accomplish this very challenging task, we have to be willing to die to the way things have been. This is the only way that we can finally step out of the illusion of the personal, the illusion of being a unique individual. But we live in a world where we are so invested in the idea of being unique that it's a heroic task to even begin to consider what it could mean to give that up. Only when we dare to allow ourselves to directly perceive the impersonal nature of *every aspect* of our own personal experience can anything truly change. Why? Because then we will have seen through the biggest illusion there is.

It is the presence or absence of ego that defines our relationship to our experience. For example, we could have a profound spiritual experience and yet because of the compulsive need to personalize, our *perception* of what occurred would be distorted. The habit of personalization distorts our perception of almost everything that we experience because of the ego's unending need to see itself in a particular way. But a mind that is enlightened experiences perception that is undistorted *because it is empty of that which is personal.*

Clear perception, perception that is free from the distorting influence of personalization, cannot reveal itself as long as we are invested in seeing ourselves as being unique. Only the individual who sincerely wants to be free will know the enormity of renunciation that is required for the mind to become liberated from the pull of ego. In order to directly experience that extraordinary quality of mind, all attachment to the personal must burn away in the renunciate fire that is the passion for Liberation. That fire has to burn until there is no longer any compulsion to locate oneself through this habit of personalizing that which was never personal.

Sustained contemplation of the impersonal nature of all personal experience requires tremendous strength of character and an unbridled passion for Liberation. Without that passion, the intensity of interest that is required to see through the illusion of the personal will not be sustained. Very few succeed in liberating themselves from the overwhelming temptation that the illusion of the personal creates. To be victorious, one has to have enough strength to stand alone in one's own experience without needing to personalize it. Indeed, to succeed in liberating ourselves from ignorance and delusion, we have to get to that point where we're able to directly perceive the impersonal nature of every aspect of our own personal experience.

Many mistakenly assume that a perspective that is impersonal is inherently cold and devoid of human qualities. But nothing could be further from the truth. Impersonal does not mean inhuman. Impersonal means free from the inherent distortion that is always created by that which is personal. Once again, the habitual movement to personalize is ego, and its fundamental motive is to see itself as being separate at all times, in all places, through all circumstances. This movement of separation is inherently destructive because it is *always* antithetical to the conscious realization of our true Self.

The courageous willingness to unconditionally renounce this very personal relationship to our own experience is what enables the true Self to freely manifest itself *as ourselves*. It is imperative to recognize the fact that the true Self *could never be personal or unique*. And the degree to which we are able to renounce the need to see our own experience as being personal or unique will be the same degree to which the true Self will become manifest.

When the true Self is able to *freely* express itself, only then will the depth of our humanity reveal itself in all its fullness and glory. In that individual who has freed him- or herself from the distortion of the personal, that impersonal depth can be instantly recognized as flawless spontaneity, overwhelming compassion and fearless clarity.

Cultivating the presence of mind necessary to recognize the ultimately impersonal nature of all human experience requires a deep and sustained practice of introspection, contemplation and meditation. That attainment enables one who is sincere to eradicate all obstacles to clear perception. The task is a solitary one. One can only do this for oneself. And only if we want to be free more than anything else will we have the integrity of interest necessary to liberate ourselves from the deadly illusion that attachment to that which is personal always creates.

the fifth tenet
For the Sake of the Whole

The first tenet, *Clarity of Intention,* tells us that if we are going to make any real progress in spiritual life, it's essential that we cultivate the intention to be free to such a degree that our own Enlightenment becomes more important to us than anything else in this world. But the fifth tenet tells us something altogether different. It tells us that to become liberated only for our own sake is selfish. The fifth tenet tells us that what is of the greatest importance is that our passion for Liberation be not only for our own sake but *for the sake of the whole.* For the sake of the whole means Liberation not for ourselves, but for everyone else.

Most seekers are interested in Enlightenment only for their own sake, only for their own *personal* Liberation. Indeed, when we begin the spiritual life, the most important thing to us is our own happiness, our own personal experience of expanded states of consciousness, our own Enlightenment. But there comes a time when some seekers begin to recognize that spiritual experience is not only for their own welfare. Because they have gone deeply into the spiritual experience, they have discovered something sacred. It is the recognition of an obligation, an obligation that literally commands them to cease to live for themselves alone, and instead to live for the sake of the whole. In that obligation it not only becomes apparent that this life is not our own in any personal sense, but it also becomes clear that true Liberation can be found only when this life is lived not for our own happiness, but in the service of a cause that is always greater than ourselves.

The fifth tenet makes clear that to live the spiritual life in earnest always means ceasing to live only for ourselves. Not even personal Liberation, it tells us, is the main event of spiritual life. The fifth tenet says that, in fact, the entire purpose of spiritual experience is, in the end, the simple yet all-encompassing recognition that the meaning and significance of human life is never found through having or getting for ourselves, but only through *giving*. Indeed, the experience of being alive only begins to make sense, *absolute, perfect sense,* when there is not even a trace of doubt left about this question.

But relatively few get to this point because most seekers are only looking for a way to be happy. They want to find a way to alleviate their own suffering. They want to *personally* be able to experience a permanent state of peace, joy and bliss. And they hope that the experience of bliss will enable them to be impervious to all suffering.

The fifth tenet, *For the Sake of the Whole,* calls the seeker to address this self-centered position through inquiring very deeply into the question: *What is life really all about?* Is this event, this experience of embodied consciousness, only for ourselves? Are we here only to have and to get? As seekers of Enlightenment—seekers of peace, clarity and simplicity of being—are we trying to get something only for ourselves? Or is there, in fact, a deeper understanding of life and the meaning of spiritual experience that finally liberates us from self-concern?

The fifth tenet tells us that what is more important than even our own Enlightenment is the conscious recognition of a profound sense of obligation. What emerges from the recognition of that obligation is a mysterious and passionate sense of care for the whole. And this passionate care is larger than anything that can be called personal. Indeed, its nature is impersonal and its intensity always overwhelms all that is personal within us. This passion wants order where there is disorder, wholeness where there is division, truth where there is falsehood and love where there is hate.

The ego can appreciate the first four tenets. It finds them perfectly reasonable. But upon hearing the fifth tenet, the ego says, "That's it! Enough is *enough!*" The ego hates the fifth tenet because it recognizes, in a way that is unequivocal, that in that passionate, impersonal care for the whole, it has absolutely nothing to gain and everything to lose.

The fifth tenet tells us never to see our own Liberation outside the context of everyone else's Liberation. *"Cease to live for yourself alone,"* it says. *"For the sake of the whole, liberate yourself from all self-concern."* When you get to that point in your own evolution where you recognize that there is nothing to do that makes any sense except to wholeheartedly give your own life so that it can be lived for the sake of the whole, Liberation *will* be the result. But at that point it's no longer the most important thing. Liberation, *personal* Liberation, will be the automatic result of no longer living for yourself, but within the context of the fifth tenet, it's no longer the main event.

So many of us experience profound difficulty simply coming to terms with the life we are living. It seems that we're endlessly trying to get away from it. We feel uncomfortable with the body that we have, uncomfortable with our memories, and we are ever struggling with the movement of our own thoughts and emotions. That's why we are always trying to overcome the past, rearrange the present and control the future. That's why we are seeking Enlightenment— because we are craving relief.

If we cease to live for our own sake, we will indeed experience relief, but not the kind of relief we had bargained for. You see, in ceasing to live for ourselves alone, we assume a great burden. And that burden is the evolution of the whole. Wholeheartedly assuming that burden instantly liberates the individual from the weight of the personal and simultaneously enables him or her to be available, to respond, to give in a way that was previously inconceivable.

When it no longer makes any sense to you to live only for yourself, something mysterious and utterly liberating will occur. You will discover that this life, your own life—with your own memory, lived in your own body, with your very own thoughts and your very own emotions—will suddenly make *perfect* sense. The "you" who you are right now will be recognized as being perfect *as it is.* It will become obvious that you are in *exactly* the right place, at the right time, for the right reasons, doing the right thing—*just as you are.*

Now there is a sense of being deeply at home and connected with life in a way that is inconceivably profound yet completely ordinary. The "home" I'm referring to is where *you* (the personal you—the body, memory and mind that you have right now) and *life*—LIFE ABSOLUTE—merge and become ONE. Suddenly everything fits. *You are exactly where you're supposed to be,* being the person who you already are and always have been—that very same person who you were always trying to get away from.

The more you care about others and the less you care about yourself, the clearer this experience of being at home will be. When you begin to care about the greater good more than you care about yourself, all the problems that you thought you had will disappear. Everything you thought you had to overcome in order to become a better person will suddenly seem insignificant and even irrelevant. All the experiences you thought you needed to have in order to feel complete will appear to be empty and superficial. When you give everything that you have and everything that you are to everyone else, there will be nothing left for you. And that *nothing* that is left *is* your Liberation. When you give everything, you are not separate from the source of life itself.

In the beginning there was *nothing*. Then for no apparent reason, from nothing suddenly *something* was born. From pure emptiness the whole universe of life sprang into being. In that instant there was a big "YES!" That same unlimited consciousness embodied *as you* is that very same *something,* that same "YES!" that continuously arises from nothing. If you truly want to be free, you must understand that from this vast perspective, ego consciousness and self-concern— *even concern for your own Liberation*—are the expression of a fundamental denial of who and what you *already* are.

When you cease to live for yourself, when you give everything you have and everything you are *for the sake of the whole,* that's the end of it. It's the end of you as you've known yourself to be. It's the end of becoming. It's the end of having a problem that you need to overcome. It's even the end of striving for Enlightenment. It's the end of all of that and the beginning of an unconditional response to life that says "YES!" and that only gives.

When you stop trying to get anything back for yourself, you will find yourself immersed in an unending revelation of perfect Liberation here and now—always and forever being who you already are.

.

Desire:
The Perennial Obstacle

The Promise of Perfection

The Promise of Perfection

illusion

We often hear teachers of Enlightenment confidently inform us that what we are seeing is not real. To describe this state of affairs, they insist that much of what we perceive is an illusion. This can be very difficult to understand. Indeed, it is confusing when we are told that we're not seeing things clearly, we're not seeing things as they are. So what *does* it mean when teachers of Enlightenment tell us that most of the time what we are perceiving is not as it appears?

If something is illusory, it means that it does not exist. It means that what we are perceiving has no independent self-existence outside of our own mind and field of sensory experience. It means, therefore, that what we are experiencing is something that we are creating with our own mind and senses and then projecting upon the world around us. Most of us, even though we're rarely aware of it, live a great deal of our lives very much lost in and distracted by psychological and sensory perceptions that have no objective reality.

What creates this almost perfect continuity of illusion, this unreal stream of thought and sense perception? It is the end-less wanting, the endless craving for personal gratification.

wanting

You see, in this world, the world of the ego, the world of the separate personal self, it is *wanting*—wanting this and wanting that—that generates so much excitement, anticipation and intense longing. It is important to become aware of the fact that when we want something or want someone, we experience ourselves as being intensely alive because it is then that we feel in touch with the drive within us to *have*. This drive to have—"I want for *me,* I want for *myself*"—is experienced by the ego as a positive thing. And when we think about whatever it is that we want—a new house, a new car—it *excites* us. And it is this very excitement that distorts our perception.

It's easy to get in touch with the significance of what I'm speaking about if we look into what it means to want another human being. When we intensely desire another person, who we perceive that person to be in the midst of that longing is infinitely more than who he or she actually is. When we fall in love, we find the mere presence of the other intoxicating. Just to look at that person is mesmerizing. But after we get to know him or her intimately, we discover that it's very difficult to sustain that same level of intoxication. We still find that person attractive, we still feel affection, but that *special* something, that magic, is gone.

In the same way, if we decide we're going to buy a new car, we will find ourselves thinking about it very often. When we see that car, we will experience a thrill. Just looking at it will make us feel special. And when we anticipate the moment when we are finally going to have it for ourselves, we will experience even more excitement.

I'm trying to bring to light why it is that certain objects in consciousness can easily appear to be more than they actually are. Precisely because both the car and the one we long to possess are objects of our desire, we see something extra, we see *more* than what is there. And that *more* that we are seeing has very little to do with the object itself. That more that we are seeing comes from our own mind, from our own imagination. What we are imagining is what we are adding to the picture. And it is what we are adding that makes our nerves dance and our hearts beat a little bit faster.

We may have walked by that window with the new car in it every day for a year. But then, one day, *bang!* Something happens. Suddenly we find ourselves seeing it differently. Before, we didn't notice it, but now something has shifted inside us, and because of this, that particular car has become *very special.* It works the same way with people. You can see a certain person every day, and then suddenly, in an instant, something can shift. It's the very same person, but now *everything* has changed. It's revealing to see that, from a certain point of view, the experience with the car and the experience with the one we long to possess are not that different.

As I said, illusion means that we are experiencing something with our mind and senses that does not actually exist. We are creating it. We are not seeing the car as it truly is; we are not seeing the one we long to possess as he or she truly is. What we are seeing is our own imagination fueled by the weight of our desire.

the promise of perfection

When that magical something happens, when suddenly the car is not just a car but "the car I *want*," or when the one we long to possess is not just whoever he or she is but "the person I *want*," in that moment and in all the moments that follow, a very significant part of what it is that we're experiencing has nothing to do with the object itself. What we're experiencing is the power of our own desire to create the illusion of perfection. When you want that car, when you really want that car but don't yet have it and can only stand in front of the window and look at it, it's not just a nice car—there's something about that car that is *magnetic*. And in that magnetism is a promise—*a promise of perfection, a* promise of perfect fulfillment. It's the same experience when the object of our desire is another human being.

You see, what is so captivating about the kind of experience that I've been describing is *not* the having of the individual or the car, because once we are finally able to possess the object of our desire, we usually experience a process of gradual or even immediate disillusionment. The whole point is that the most thrilling part of the entire process is *the wanting itself.*

Once again, for the ego, the wanting, in and of itself, is always perceived to be a positive thing. That is why it's such a shock when we experience the literally enlightening recognition that our moments of greatest joy, our moments of deepest peace and real happiness, are those when we want *nothing.* Therefore, if we want to be truly happy, we must begin to question what our relationship to the promise of perfection actually is.

the challenge

To see clearly, to see things as they are, free from illusion, is the goal of spiritual practice. It's not that difficult to experience insight now and again. It's not even that unusual for serious seekers to have an experience of transcendence if that's what they really want. But to see clearly, to see things as they really are, is something else altogether. Only that rare individual who wants to be free more than anything else and who wants to know the truth more than anything else will have the power of discrimination necessary to see through that which is unreal. For without that passion for Liberation, we will inevitably be too invested in the ever-intoxicating experience of wanting. You see, *we don't want to not want.* And this is what the problem is.

Many people say that they want to be happy, but it couldn't be true. Why? Because to experience real happiness, we have to be willing to abandon the wanting. *It's only when the wanting falls away that we can begin to experience a fullness that is always there.* You can be a very intelligent person and still be completely lost in the thrill of wanting. And the whole point is that as long as we allow ourselves to be hypnotically distracted by that thrill, we will never be able to see things clearly, we will never be able to see things as they really are.

There are times when it counts a lot more than others that we are able to see clearly—especially those moments when we experience that wanting with the greatest intensity. Those are the moments that count the most because when we want something that badly, we may be willing to do anything in order to have it. We may even be willing to deceive ourselves and others in order to be able to possess the object of our desire. In those moments, the wanting can be so compelling, so thrilling, that we may be unable to resist. Will we, in the midst of that intensity, be able to see through it?

our fundamental relationship to life

If we want to be able to see clearly, we have to be willing to look into our fundamental relationship to life. And when we do, we will discover the all-pervasive nature of desire. We will see that almost every action that we take is motivated by wanting for ourselves. Indeed, this *"I want for me"* is expressed in gross and subtle ways thousands of times every single day—when we look, when we turn our heads, when we reach out. Only when we see the movement of this compulsive wanting directly will we begin to recognize it for what it actually is—a never-ending process of pain and suffering. And as we become more and more aware of the suffering inherent in this compulsive wanting, the way we perceive and interpret our experience will begin to change. There will be an awakening of profound depth and extraordinary clarity, and this awakening will occur in direct conjunction with the recognition of the true face of desire.

So if we want to see clearly, we have to look into our fundamental relationship to life. We have to be willing to come to terms with the fact that, for most of us, it is based on what is, in the end, a very greedy and selfish wanting only for ourselves. Through having the courage to experience this fully, a door to another possibility, another way of being, will open. In fact, as a direct result, we will experience over and over again the always enlightening discovery that real happiness is found only when we want *absolutely nothing*.

The pain of wanting creates an almost endless experience of tension. And deep peace and profound sanity are found only when that tension ceases. The wanting and all of the tension inherent in it, which before we perceived as pleasure, we now recognize to be pain. This recognition has extraordinary significance because it is the beginning of a completely different relationship to life. It is the dawning of awakening.

The Psychology
of Liberation

An Absolute Relationship to Life

What Is the Ultimate Truth?

An Absolute Relationship to Life

Spiritual experiences, as profound as they may be, usually do not, in and of themselves, lastingly enlighten. Nor do they, in most cases, deeply transform our relationship to the three fundamental yet most confusing aspects of the human experience: the movement of time, the arising of thought and the presence of feeling.

It is our always conditioned and deeply compulsive relationship to these three fundamental components of our experience that creates the painful prison of illusion that is ego.

If we want to liberate ourselves from the almost unending experience of isolation and separation that this illusion creates, it is essential to begin the one-pointed contemplation of our relationship to the movement of time, the arising of thought and the presence of feeling. This contemplation, when embarked upon with sincerity and commitment, can ultimately bring us to a profound understanding of what I call *an absolute relationship to life*—which is what the enlightened relationship to time, thought and feeling actually is. Without an absolute relationship to life, there can never be any final victory over the ego's overwhelming power to ensnare us in illusion and falsehood.

time

The first component of an absolute relationship to life is our relationship to time and the movement of time.

Most of us spend our entire lives trapped—trapped and suffocating in a kind of limbo—trapped because, without even knowing it, we are *always waiting*. And that waiting is an experience of almost unbroken tyranny. We are trapped by the movement of time because we live in a constant state of anticipation—waiting, endlessly waiting, for the future to arrive. We live in this way because we believe that in the future our lives will somehow be better than they are now.

When our relationship to life is based upon waiting, it's not possible for us to know what it's like to be truly alive— because no matter what we may experience in the present moment, *we will continue to wait*. We won't stop waiting even when we experience profound happiness because, without realizing it, we will already be anticipating its demise. And in the very same way, when we experience fear and insecurity, we will also be waiting—waiting for that unpleasant experience to come to an end.

You see, on the most fundamental level we are *always* holding ourselves back. Because of this, we are unwilling to truly give, unable to trust and rarely ready to wholeheartedly engage with life. Indeed, if we look deeply, all we will see is waiting—waiting for things to change, waiting to let go. Waiting is the never-ending meantime in which our entire lives unfold.

But there is a way out. And that way out is an absolute relationship to time. An absolute relationship to time is one in which we have *stopped waiting*.

If we truly want to be free, simply through the sincere contemplation of what an absolute relationship to time means, we can liberate ourselves from the prison of waiting that we have chosen to live in. You see, in this contemplation, it soon will become clear that there is nothing to wait for. In fact, what will eventually reveal itself is the profound recognition that *there is only one moment*—and this moment *now* always is and could only ever be that one moment. Indeed, when we discover this for ourselves, we will know without any doubt that there never has been anything to wait for—not even the experience of recognizing that there was nothing to wait for! When we see this clearly, we *simply stop waiting*. And when we stop waiting, everything changes.

An absolute relationship to time is one in which we have

stopped waiting absolutely—stopped waiting for anything more to occur in order to fully *be.*

thought

The second component of an absolute relationship to life is our relationship to thought and the arising of thought.

If we want to be free, it is essential that we begin to question the fundamental beliefs that our relationship to thought is based on. As we will eventually realize for ourselves, our potential for Liberation is, in the end, entirely dependent on the kind of relationship that we have with thought.

The primary conviction that ignorance or unenlightenment is based on is the unquestioned assumption that *thought is self.* Indeed, for those of us lost in ignorance, it is in thought and the arising of thought that we experience the most intimate sense of who we are. But as all true seekers will discover, the fundamental mistake that we endlessly make is *assuming* that the content of thought has inherent reality, meaning and significance.

If we sincerely aspire to be liberated from the tyranny of ego, from the nightmarish existence of the separate sense of self, then that liberation rests on the explosive recognition that thought is not self, that thought is *only* thought. This discovery—that thought has no inherent significance except that which we *choose* to give it—is the essential insight on which liberation from ignorance and unenlightenment depends.

Like pictures in a photo album, thoughts in and of themselves, when seen objectively, are recognized as being nothing more than abstract representations of historical events. Ceasing to make the pivotal error of believing thought to be inherently real instantly reveals the truth—that who we are always has been free from and prior to the awareness of thought. This profound discovery is the birth of a radical awakening from the endless dream of ignorance and unenlightenment that so much of human life is an expression of.

Lost in and helplessly distracted by thought and the arising of thought, most of us spend our entire lives alienated from our own depths and, as a result, often experience a puzzling sense of separation from the world in which we live. It's important to understand that our unrecognized compulsive and mechanical identification with thought leaves no room in our awareness for anything other than thought. And it is the unquestioned assumption that thought is self that creates the seamless continuity of a painful illusion, which, for too many of us, literally defines the very life that we live. In the sincere quest for emancipation from that which is unreal, sooner or later thought will be revealed to be what it is—utterly empty of any inherent significance.

An absolute relationship to thought is one in which the understanding that thought is not self is never forgotten.

feeling

The third component of an absolute relationship to life is our relationship to the presence of feeling.

In the sincere quest for Liberation, quiet introspection will reveal that the fundamental perspective that we have on the experience of being alive is almost always influenced in an essential way by how we feel. For example, whenever we experience happiness, in the form of peace, joy or bliss, under the influence of those uplifting emotions, we have confidence in the fact that being alive is a very positive thing. In that happy state, everything seems possible. But when the influence of those uplifting emotions is gone and we experience insecurity—in the form of fear, anger or despair—we can easily doubt that life is worth living. Indeed, in the presence of unpleasant feelings, it will probably seem to us that the possibility of radical transformation is nothing but a distant fantasy.

A relationship to our emotional experience that is not absolute is one in which the fundamental perspective that we have on the experience of being alive is always changing according to the way we feel. If we want to see clearly, it is imperative that we begin to observe the relationship between our feeling states and the way that we perceive not only our inner experience but also the world around us.

It is illuminating when we discover for ourselves the degree to which our perspective shifts in relationship to our changing emotional states. We find that when we experience joy, there is enormous room inside our hearts for others, but when we experience fear, there is rarely any concern for anyone other than our own self. It is our constant preoccupation with the feeling dimension of our experience that often makes it difficult for us to see clearly beyond that which is merely personal. It is also the principal cause of our inability to consistently sustain a vast perspective on *all* of our experience. Unwittingly, we allow many of the conclusions that we draw about the nature of reality as a whole to be overly influenced by the way that we happen to feel. Indeed, if we are not paying close attention, in retrospect we will find that most of those conclusions were inaccurate.

Only if we want to be free more than anything else will we know that singularity of vision that has the power to manifest an absolute relationship to the unpredictable movement of feelings and emotions. An absolute relationship to feeling is rooted in the desire for freedom alone. It is that one desire that enables those who are most sincere to consistently maintain a vast perspective on all of their experience. They will be the rare ones among us because they will not lose that perspective in the tumultuous sea of ever-changing emotions.

An absolute relationship to the presence of feeling is one in which our interest in Liberation is always more important than our emotional experience.

What Is the Ultimate Truth?

Without being aware of it, most of us are convinced at the very core of our being that something is terribly wrong. And it is this one fundamental conviction that keeps us locked in the three-dimensional prison of time, thought and feeling.

If we are seeking Liberation, if we want to be free from that prison, we have to be ready to question the validity of that conviction as if our salvation depended on it—*because it does.* In the end, the difference between Enlightenment and unenlightenment completely depends on whether we have freed ourselves from the fundamental conviction that something is wrong. But the problem is that we are usually so closely identified with this conviction that it is all but impossible for us to recognize it. If this is true, and if we sincerely want to free ourselves from the bondage of that conviction and the long shadow that it casts upon our entire existence, then what are we to do?

When we want to see our way through fundamental

confusion, there is only one solution. We have to be willing to *let everything be as it is*. We have to be ready to *unconditionally* let everything be as it is. What does that mean? It means that if we want to know for ourselves what is ultimately true, we first have to be willing to let go of absolutely everything—everything we have thought, everything we have felt, everything we have desired and everything we have feared. If we can do this—simply let *everything* be—we will sink, slowly but surely, naturally and effortlessly, to the very ground of being itself. Through doing only this, letting everything be, we will find a place that is completely still, where there is no movement whatsoever. In that place there is freedom from time and thought, from the desire for pleasure and the fear of pain. In that place there is only peace. Perfect peace and a mystery that the mind cannot comprehend.

When we let everything be in this way, we take absolutely no position in relationship to anything we experience. We are resting. We are no longer struggling to maintain or control anything. We are only resting and nothing more. Finally at peace, we are utterly free from everything we have ever known—including the fundamental conviction that something is terribly wrong. The world of opposites and differences having long fallen away, there is only THAT.

Now, having transcended all opposites and resting in eternity beyond the mind, what *is* the ultimate truth? Having gone beyond time, having gone beyond becoming, resting in a place that existed before the universe was born, there is only one truth—*nothing ever happened.* At that extraordinary depth, that's what the truth is. And it is that profound discovery—that nothing ever happened—that *is* Enlightenment.

When we return to the world of time, thought and feeling, the power of that revelation, if it has been deep enough, has the miraculous potential to completely liberate us from all the historically based, life-inhibiting impressions that have been made on our consciousness. It was our absolute conviction in the significance of those painful impressions that created the estrangement from our own deepest Self. And it was that same conviction that convinced us that something fundamental was terribly wrong. But when that revelation has made a deep enough impression on our consciousness—when we finally do come home to our true Self—the past is literally destroyed.

So what does the liberating discovery that nothing ever happened mean upon our return to the world? It means that *nothing is wrong!*

Beyond time, beyond the world of opposites and differences, where nothing ever happened, what the ultimate truth is, is a mystery. But *in* the world of opposites and differences, where many things are always happening, what is the truth *there?* The answer to that all-important question entirely depends upon how deep and profound our own experience has been. For if our experience has been ultimately superficial, lacking the knowledge of that radical depth, if we've only known the world of becoming and have not tasted the timeless, that mystery from which the world of becoming arose, then it's more than likely that the truth of our own experience will be based on the fundamental conviction that something is terribly wrong. Never having tasted that eternal ground that is always untouched by anything that has ever happened, all we can know in our human experience is a happiness that is fleeting and a deep conviction that life itself is fundamentally limited. But when we have known that ground of being, even if it was only for a few moments, we will never be able to forget it. Indeed, that experience will inevitably determine that the deepest conviction upon which our life is based is that *nothing is wrong*. This is very important. Whether we are aware of it or not, our deepest experience of life always exerts a pivotal *positive or negative* influence upon the way we perceive the world.

If we want to be free and seek that freedom through the knowledge of what is ultimately true, then we must make the effort to find out what fundamental conviction exerts the greatest influence on the way we perceive the world. We must sincerely ask ourselves: Is that conviction ultimately positive or negative? And once we've answered that question, then we must ask ourselves: How deep is the experience that that conviction is based upon?

Embracing
Heaven & Earth

Meditation Is a Metaphor for Enlightenment

Perils of the Path

Liberation without a Face

The Glory of God

The Call of the Absolute

These five chapters endeavor to bring to light the true meaning and significance of nonduality. *They attempt to reveal the deeply mysterious relationship and simultaneous nondifference between heaven and earth, between Enlightenment and the human experience.*

Meditation Is a Metaphor
for Enlightenment

When sitting in meditation, it is important to be still and not to move. *Relax* as much as possible. Be at ease and free from tension, but at the same time *be alert*. Do not concentrate on any particular point. Allow your attention to become vast, wide and deep.

Not moving is a metaphor for the enlightened state. One who has realized the goal of Liberation is one who never moves, never strays. Even though that individual may appear to walk and talk, to respond to life just like everybody else, inwardly he or she *never* moves. That is why it's important to be still, to be *completely* still.

Profound relaxation and freedom from existential tension is the foundation for extraordinary transformation. Deep relaxation is not simply a pleasant state to be attained but is the very ground of Enlightenment.

It doesn't matter if thoughts come and go, it doesn't matter if feelings come and go, and it doesn't even matter if ecstasy comes and goes. The only thing that matters is not moving, remaining completely at ease and being fully awake.

Some people say that when we meditate, we shouldn't move physically. Others say that when we meditate, our minds shouldn't wander. But the not moving I'm speaking about is deeper than that. It means never straying from our true nature.

Sooner or later after entering the path, we will have the liberating experience of wanting nothing and needing nothing. That is when we discover what our true nature is all about. That is when we fall deep within the Self. Like falling into the mouth of a volcano, down and down and down we go, sinking so deep that we even forget about the falling. When this happens, there is inexpressible contentment because one recognizes that there is absolutely nothing missing.

The only way to understand what Enlightenment is, is to experience for yourself a mystery that cannot be imagined and a depth that cannot be measured. In that depth, you will find out what it's like to want nothing at all. In that freedom from wanting, there is a peace so profound that the greatest challenge is simply not moving away from it. When I speak about not moving, *this* is what I'm referring to.

Moving away takes various shapes and forms. One form that it takes is the deeply held conviction that something is wrong. This one catches almost everybody. When something is wrong, we want to find a way to fix it, and we abandon our seat in order to find a solution. Through the act of seeking a solution, unknowingly we wander away from where we were. But if we had resisted the temptation to do so, we would never have left that place that is free from wanting, which is where we were before we became convinced that there was a problem we needed to overcome.

As we look inside ourselves with more and more depth, we will see this desire to move away. We will see that this desire is the primordial impulse to *become,* which, for most of us, is all that we know. The impulse to become is antithetical to the unimaginable perfection of the peace we have discovered. You see, unconsciously, subconsciously and even consciously we're always running away from that place of perfect peace. To where? To where we *think* we want to be.

So if we want to experience meditation, if we want to know that which answers every question but which the mind cannot comprehend, we must learn to resist the temptation to move away. The greatest challenge for the individual who wants to be free more than anything else is not to experience the truth—which is the explosive recognition that one has never been away from home—but it is the heroic practice of ceaselessly resisting the temptation to ever move away from that truth.

Unless we can succeed in liberating ourselves from the compulsive need to move away—which is the desire to have, to become—it will be impossible to experience the kind of depth that I'm speaking about for more than an instant. Indeed, a life that expresses true Liberation is a life in which we have not only *experienced* this depth, this stillness, this inconceivable fullness, but are permanently abiding there. Unless, when we turn within, we're willing to leave the world behind in a way that is bold and fearless, the likelihood of a radical transformation actually occurring is very small.

It's important to understand that for the ego, for that part of ourselves that only wants to be separate, not moving represents dissolution and death. You see, not moving ultimately returns us to that profound and mysterious place where we were before we were born, before creation ever occurred. And the whole point of meditation is to experience that place, to know that ineffable mystery that reveals itself when we've left the world far behind, *while being fully created, fully human.* That means not avoiding in any way the mysterious implications of this paradox. When we have tasted the end of becoming, which is the extraordinary experience of perfect peace, even if only temporarily, our understanding of what it means to be a human being changes dramatically.

When meditation is deep and profound, *that which is created recognizes itself to be that which is uncreated.* It is only then that our potential for Enlightenment reveals itself. But when we see ourselves to be only that which is created, that which is in a constant state of becoming, we will remain unconscious of our own unlimited depth. As long as we see ourselves to be only that which is in a constant state of becoming, all we will know is perpetual movement and endless striving.

But when we recognize ourselves to be that which is uncreated, the perpetual striving to become *ceases.* That's when our perspective undergoes a radical shift. In an instant it becomes deep, vast and limitless. The radical transformation that is Enlightenment occurs when we recognize ourselves to be that which is created *and* that which is uncreated *and never move from that realization.* It is only the knowing of that which is uncreated in the midst of creation that makes it possible to be free in this world.

Meditation can be the door to the direct experience of this kind of unconditional freedom. The way it works is not complicated. The discovery and recognition of that which is uncreated, *supported by the renunciation of the compulsive need to become,* liberates those who are truly sincere from the tyrannical grip of the ego. It is then that the pure conscious intelligence that is the source *and* expression of life begins to manifest its own true nature—which is love. There is no why to this. This love, which is inconceivable, simply is. And it can be known only when the ceaseless striving to have and to become has been transcended.

That's why when we sit in meditation, it's so important to be still and not to move.

Perils of the Path

The greatest peril of the path for those who seek Enlightenment is not leaving enough room inside themselves for what they do not know. And the greatest peril of the path for those who already are enlightened is neglecting to leave enough room inside themselves for what they do not know.

If we want to know what Enlightenment is, then we have to leave infinite room inside ourselves for *what we do not already know.* That simply means that no matter what we *think* we understand, if we want to directly experience that profound depth of Self, the discovery of which always liberates, then we have to create infinite room inside ourselves for what we do not know.

The reason we have so much difficulty experiencing enlightened perception—which is seeing beyond the mind and knowing beyond memory—is simply because we don't leave enough room inside ourselves for what we do not know. And the reason we don't leave enough room inside ourselves for what we do not know is that without being aware of it, we believe we *already* know. Already know what? Already know *everything*—including what it is that we don't know!

Already knowing is how the ego protects itself from the unknown. From the perspective of Enlightenment, already knowing is what the ego is. Ego is the veneer of invulnerability and overconfidence that creates a life-numbing wall of separation. A wall of separation that always divides the domain of experience into two: inner and outer, self and other, individual and world.

From the perspective of Enlightenment, the very definition of ego is *arrogance*. The arrogance of already knowing. The invulnerable overconfidence of already knowing is the fortress of limitation that always keeps the unknown at bay. From the perspective of Enlightenment, the unknown is a metaphor for no limitation, and no limitation is a description of the experience of consciousness liberated from the inherently limiting arrogance of already knowing.

Not knowing is synonymous with enlightened consciousness because not knowing automatically creates infinite room for the unknown, which is experienced as consciousness liberated from any sense of limitation. *Humility* is the human face of enlightened consciousness precisely because that face has been freed from the arrogance of already knowing. Humility is the direct consequence of always first *not knowing* in relationship to all experience. *Arrogance* or ego is the human face of unenlightened consciousness because it is the direct consequence of always first *already knowing* in relationship to all experience. In not knowing there is always infinite room for the unknown, but in already knowing there never could be.

But the nature of Enlightenment is paradoxical. Its perfect continuity rests upon a delicate balance of opposites. On one hand, enlightened consciousness is a direct consequence of abiding in a state where there is always infinite room for the unknown. And on the other hand, the very stability of that consciousness equally rests upon a doubtless conviction, a *knowing* of the ultimate nature of reality that is unshakable.

So therefore, the tremendous challenge for all true seekers of enlightened perception lies in finding that perfect middle place between knowing and not knowing and, having found it, *staying there.*

Once again, the greatest peril for those who seek Enlightenment is not leaving room inside themselves for what they do not know. And the greatest peril for those who already are enlightened is making the very same mistake. Indeed, the reason that deep spiritual experiences often have such confusing results is that they have the potential to bestow a powerful knowing or strong conviction that may be unsupported by a deep and continuous surrender to the unknown. This is the most precarious aspect of Enlightenment and of spiritual experience in general: arrogance or already knowing tainting the potentially immaculate expression of powerfully awakened consciousness. This is why Enlightenment is such a delicate business. Unless we hit the bull's eye—which means that perfect middle place between knowing and not knowing—the result of profound spiritual experiences, *including even Enlightenment itself,* will inevitably be imperfect. That simply means that in the one who is enlightened, a shadow of ego will remain because in his or her attainment, *knowing* will be more powerful than *not knowing.* That is why the pursuit of Enlightenment is such a delicate matter for the seeker *and* finder—it is so easy to err on one side or the other.

If seekers are unwilling to surrender all prior knowing, then the liberating power of enlightened perception will remain ever beyond their grasp because, without that inconceivable leap into the unknown, the confidence of knowing that mystery that abides beyond the mind will always be unstable. And for those rare individuals who have found, those who have taken that leap, now that they are finders, will there *still* be room inside them for what they don't know? Once confidence in Enlightenment has finally been won, will the all-important humility still be there? Or will the finder have become trapped in one side of the paradox, now being only *the one who knows?*

Once you *know,* and once you know that you know, there's no going back. That's why the greatest danger for the finder is doubtlessness—even though doubtlessness is an essential ingredient of Liberation.

You see, in the end, the goal for seekers and finders is the same: to always leave room inside themselves for what they do not know, to manifest an attainment that casts no shadow, to rest always in that perfect middle place between all pairs of opposites.

Liberation without a Face

Perennial knowledge has always told us that *ego* is the one and only obstacle to Liberation. What is ego? Ego is the sense of one's self as being *separate*. Ego is the part of ourselves that sees itself as separate from the other, separate from the world and separate from the whole universe. The ego will use *any* opportunity to position itself in order to be able to see itself as being separate from the other. And one of the most significant ways that we see ourselves as being separate is in relationship to gender and sexual orientation.

Our experience of being either male or female is almost always pregnant with countless unexamined ideas—ideas about how we should be, how we want to be, how others believe we should be and how we imagine others want us to be. And more often than not, most of our ideas about what it means to be a man or what it means to be a woman are based on conformity to fixed and rigid beliefs or are the defiant expression of rebellion against them—no matter what our sexual orientation. We almost always experience a great deal of insecurity in relationship to the profoundly confusing question of gender identity and sexual orientation, and knowingly or unknowingly most of us struggle for our entire lives to live up to these beliefs. But because we rarely question for ourselves what it could mean to be *free* in relationship to the whole issue of gender and sexual orientation, we usually remain lost in a hall of mirrors, our attention helplessly riveted to images that keep us bound to a painfully separate sense of self. So, what is the relationship between Enlightenment and gender? What is the relationship between spiritual freedom and sexual orientation?

In the revelation of Enlightenment, who and what we are is discovered to be beyond *any* concept of difference, including male or female. But most significant of all, we come upon a liberating perspective that powerfully transcends the movement toward conformity or rebellion. And in the end, it is only through discovering that perspective directly for ourselves that the path of true freedom can be found.

If we want to be free, it is imperative to recognize that the ego—which is the separate sense of self—will use any and every opportunity to create the experience of a personal identity that *appears* to be unique and distinct. The words "I am a . . ." usually refer to a picture of ourselves as being unique and distinct—*whatever* that picture is. And as long as we don't want to be free more than anything else, the words that follow "I am a . . ." will signify EGO. That includes all

of the ideas we have about being male or female and whatever beliefs we attach to our sexual orientation.

So therefore, if we do want to be free more than anything
else, we have to ask ourselves: What is the relationship between
the revelation of a Self that transcends any and all notions of
difference and the actuality of being a human being in a male
body or a female body?

In order to discover the answer, we first have to understand that the enlightened state is often referred to as the
"natural" state and the unenlightened state is considered to
be unnatural in comparison. Natural means *free from existential tension*. From an energetic point of view, this existential
tension is what the ego is. And when the separate sense
of self unravels, dissipates and eventually disappears, the constant *self-conscious* tension that is experienced in the body falls
away. Enlightenment, then, is a condition that is fundamentally free from that existential tension that is ego.

So regarding the intriguing question of freedom in relationship to gender and sexual orientation, what we want to
know is: What exactly is the enlightened or *natural and
unselfconscious* expression of manhood or womanhood?
What is the natural and unselfconscious expression of sexual
orientation? If the enlightened perspective is based upon the
revelation of a self that is free from any sense of difference,
including all concepts, ideas and beliefs about gender and

sexual orientation, then what would it be like to be a man who was free from fixed ideas about what it means to be a man? What would it be like to be a woman who was free from fixed ideas about what it means to be a woman? What would it be like to be a man or a woman who was not attached to fixed ideas of being a man or woman, *yet at the same time was not in any way avoiding or denying the fact of their gender or sexual orientation?*

It would be *free from ego,* which means free from every trace of self-consciousness that would support a sense of oneself as being unique, special or separate in any way.

If it is true that at the very inner core of our being there is absolutely no notion of a separate self that can be imagined with the human mind, and yet at the same time outwardly there is a projection that is the human body, which inherently does express difference, then if we want to be free, we must find a way to express that difference without it in any way carrying the weight of ego. That would mean that in order for the expression of differences between male and female and of different sexual orientations to be utterly free from the distorting influence of ego, we must reach that point in our own spiritual evolution where we are always more interested in being free than we are in being male or female or being identified with any particular sexual orientation. The implications in this are overwhelming because they force the true seeker to heroically question his or her attachment to and identification with any notion of self that can be imagined by the mind.

The enlightened self casts no reflection in the mind of the enlightened one. That's why the universal character of enlightened consciousness is *innocence*. And true innocence will be unselfconsciously expressed when we are attached only to that part of ourselves that we cannot see, taste, smell or touch. Then and only then will the expression of our maleness, of our femaleness, of our sexual orientation be free from ego and undistorted by the need to see ourselves as being unique, special or separate in any way.

The Glory of God

What is the glory of God? What is the defining expression of that which transcends yet includes all things?

The glory of God is the shattering realization that everything is *always* perfect. The glory of God is the inherent perfection of all things at all times, in all places, through all circumstances. Even earthquakes, disease and bloody warfare —that's all the glory of God too. The glory of God is the inherent perfection of all things *as they are*. You see, from an *absolute* perspective, the eye of the Self sees only God and makes no distinctions whatsoever. Heaven and hell, good and evil, everything known and unknown, seen and unseen are *all* recognized only to be different expressions of that one inconceivable mystery beyond name and form. Beyond all pairs of opposites, the glory of God is all there is—just absolute, incomparable *perfection*.

Before time and space, before the universe was born, there was nothing. Then suddenly from nothing came something. There was an explosion, and what we all are right now—including you and me—is that explosion in motion. That explosion in motion is one radiant being—conscious, whole and undivided.

Enlightenment is the direct recognition of one's own true face as none other than that radiant being—conscious, whole and undivided. And it is the recognition of the utterly complete and *always perfect* nature of that true face that releases the sense of individuality from identification with the hypnotic grip of ego consciousness.

But there is more to Enlightenment than the liberating discovery of the inherent perfection of the absolute or non-dual nature of all things. And that is the emergence of a powerful imperative to *evolve*. When something came from nothing, and the explosion in motion that is all of life came into being, a perpetual state of *becoming* was born. In the spiritual revelation, that movement is experienced as an impersonal command from the Self to transcend, to evolve, to utterly transform this world so that it can become a dynamic, living expression of the perfection that it *already is.* This spiritually inspired passion, which arises from the Self, unleashes the fire of absolute love and ego-defying compassion into this world. It is always a force to be reckoned with. Its unceasing demand is evolution and its tangible expression is to create order out of disorder. Indeed, the boundless creativity of this evolutionary impulse in action strives to manifest higher and higher expressions of miraculous wholeness and integration.

The command to transcend and evolve that is experienced in the spiritual revelation is the unrelenting scream of the Absolute calling on all who have the ears to hear and the eyes to see to surrender wholeheartedly for the sake of that evolutionary imperative.

This ceaseless imperative to evolve is *also* the glory of God. And the greatest paradox is that that glory is both the radiant, ever full and complete, always perfect ground of all that is *and* the very foundation and essence of that explosion in motion that strives to manifest higher and higher expressions of wholeness and integration.

Enlightenment, then, is the direct realization of the dual nature of the glory of God as the inherent perfection of all things and a ceaseless imperative to evolve. In that realization, there is not only the release from the hypnotic grip of ego consciousness but also the ecstatic movement of energy that occurs only through submission to the creative principle. What is so precious about human life is our sacred potential to experience this glory in our own hearts and minds and, in so doing, become a *conscious* instrument of it.

But the evolutionary journey is a perilous one, and the blossoming of the human spirit can go terribly wrong. When the ecstatic embrace of the evolutionary imperative is not firmly grounded in the profound knowledge of the inherent perfection of all things, the consequences can be disastrous. Why? Because the ego's insidious and deadly investment in domination and control can easily be fueled by the tremendously empowering discovery of the evolutionary imperative *unless one is first firmly grounded in the awakened knowledge of the inherent perfection of all things.* Indeed, without that grounding, inspired passion easily becomes fertile ground for the ego to identify itself with that which is Absolute, thereby enabling our darkest impulses to masquerade as the greatest good.

The other great potential for confusion is when the glory of God is seen to be *only* the inherent perfection of all things devoid of *any* evolutionary imperative. Whenever this misrepresentation of the complete and paradoxical nature of the glory of God occurs, the unrestrained creative potential of the explosion in motion that is ourselves will be profoundly inhibited. And not only will it be profoundly inhibited, but in that partial perspective, the full glory of the Absolute principle is denied, depriving our own deepest Self, which is God, our unconditional participation in that glory.

Enlightenment—when it is deep and profound, vast, full and complete—always recognizes the glory of God as being simultaneously the inherent perfection of all things *and* the ceaseless imperative to evolve.

The Call of the Absolute

What do you gain when you see the face of God? The answer is simple: *absolutely nothing*. This is what we discover for ourselves in spiritual revelation. But because we have been brought up to be materialists, we assume that the purpose of life is to get, to have and to accumulate. And unknowingly, when we embark on the spiritual path, most of us bring this deeply embedded materialistic relationship to life along with us. We want a transcendent power to bestow divine grace upon us so that we can have it *for ourselves*. But what we don't know is that *that power is more materialistic than we are*. If we are lucky enough to experience its mysterious presence moving in, around and through us, we will discover the terrifying yet magnetic attraction of absolute love that asks for nothing less than everything from us. Every single breath that moves in and out of our lungs, that presence wants only for *itself*. Those who have had this experience either have been overwhelmed with ecstasy by the unimaginable intensity of its absolute nature or have become paralyzed by their own fear of it. "I want all of you for myself" is the unending call of that mystery. Those who are the luckiest among us find themselves choicelessly compelled to respond from the depths of their being when they hear that call. Even when the whole world is screaming, "No, you *mustn't* do this—you shouldn't give yourself to that which the mind cannot understand," they fall to their knees, ready and willing to die.

Spiritual experience that has the power to transform gives nothing to us; it only takes everything away. The overwhelming austerity of this simple truth, when we recognize it for ourselves, brings us to the very edge of the known. And what we discover out there at the edge is that the power of absolute love to affect this world, so overcome with self-created pain and misery, is entirely dependent upon *us*.

There is a reservoir of unimaginable strength and energy, always unknown to the mind, that flows spontaneously from the surrendered heart into this suffering world when we have responded to that call with trust rather than fear. But if we have become hypnotized by the insatiable needs of the ego, that miraculous power will either remain trapped inside us forever or, even worse, will be used to affect the world for the ego's own unwholesome purposes. Indeed, the ego can easily usurp the yearning of the spiritual heart by masquerading as that same heart if our attraction to absolute love isn't free from the desire for personal gain.

The death-defying leap into the unknown that the movement of profound surrender is, is the most powerful shift of energy and attention that can occur within human consciousness, other than the falling away of the physical form. That is why the actual consequences of that kind of leap are always so extraordinary. Once that leap has been taken, the traditional boundaries of the personality have been shattered, expanding the sphere of self-sense in all directions. The enormous risk that must be taken for this kind of transformation to occur requires a degree of courage and trust that is inconceivable to most. That risk will only be taken for one of two reasons: an intense desire to be *nobody* or an equally intense desire to be *somebody*.

The notion of surrendering to the power of absolute love is, from the ego's perspective, completely terrifying. But if the ego usurps the sincere desire for surrender in pursuit of the promise of *divine* selfhood, the result will not be a self finally free from the chains of ego, but rather an ego that has become enlightened. The power of absolute love is completely impersonal and its unending magnetic call to all who would hear it is equally impersonal. That means that that mysterious power accepts any and all who are willing to respond wholeheartedly to its call for submission—*no matter what their condition may be.*

Surrender, when it is final, instantly brings personal evolution to a halt because that individual then becomes a messenger of the divine. Whatever the motivation of the one who has taken that leap, the condition of the personality becomes fixed forever at the moment of surrender. That is why it is so important that the purification of the vehicle be sincerely and systematically cultivated—only then will the personality be released from the ego-driven desire to be somebody *prior* to the catalytic event of unconditional submission to the Absolute.

The power of absolute love is a raging fire of uncontainable majesty that consumes any and all who come too close to its flames. That fire burns wildly, aware only of *itself*. That is why the wholehearted and very *conscious* participation in the entire process of self-purification is always such an integral part of spiritual evolution and transformation. Indeed, in most cases, the extraordinary leap that profound surrender always is will not occur free from the corrupting influence of ego unless our conscious participation in our own purification is intense and deeply committed.

What is so miraculous, though, is the powerful recognition that that participation in the process of our own transformation *is* that raging fire of absolute love in action, moving in our own hearts and minds as the desire for Liberation itself.

The Impersonal Enlightenment Fellowship

Founded in 1988, the Impersonal Enlightenment Fellowship is a nonprofit organization that supports and facilitates the teaching work of Andrew Cohen. It is dedicated to the Enlightenment of the individual and the expression of Enlightenment in the world. The Impersonal Enlightenment Fellowship has centers in the United States, Europe, Australia and India.

For more information about Andrew Cohen and his teaching, and the Impersonal Enlightenment Fellowship, please contact one of the centers listed below or visit our website at www.andrewcohen.org.

Impersonal Enlightenment Fellowship
World Center
PO Box 2360
Lenox, MA 01240 USA
tel: 413-637-6000 or 800-376-3210
fax: 413-637-6015
email: ief@andrewcohen.org

Impersonal Enlightenment Fellowship London
Centre Studios
Englands Lane
London NW3 4YD UK
tel: 44-207-419-8100
fax: 44-207-419-8101
email: ieflondon@andrewcohen.org